Being Conte 1

sensitively w~~ritten exploring~~ ~~both the challenges and opportu~~-
nities for those living a spiritually single life. Through focusing on and pursuing God's call, plan and purpose for each of
our lives, Sheryl Sanderson encourages us to live a life full of
joy; finding true contentment now, in the exact time and place
where God has us.

Lana Davidson,
Missions Pastor, Riverside Community Church

As one who grew up in a spiritually divided home; as a mother who walked alongside a daughter who single-parented three
young children for ten years; and now, as a Pastor of Care and
Counsel at Riverside Community Church, I experience this issue of spiritual singleness and accompanying issues presenting so
often. I appreciate Sheryl's explanations, observations, and ap-
plications with comforting and encouraging words, along with
the validation and resolutions of her own personal journey of
spiritual singleness. This book is a good resource for many including those of us who work in caring and helping ministries.

Esther Cullen,
Pastor of Care and Counsel
at Riverside Community Church

Being Content While Spiritually Single covers all the bases. Sheryl
Sanderson is inspired and has inspired me to use this resource in
both the counselling office and my discipleship work. This book
is a one stop shop of singles questions surrounding purpose,

marriage, children and how to remain content whilst knowing there are answers. This is a resource I will come back to time after time.

David Anderson
Professional Counsellor & Discipleship Pastor
at Riverside Community Church

There are a couple of words that come to mind regarding Sheryl's latest book-timely and sensitive. The issues discussed in these pages are of great importance to the modern church and the realities it faces. And with typical Sheryl grace, they are approached with wisdom, thoughtfulness, and gentleness.

Terry Janzsen,
Senior Pastor, Riverside Community Church

Being Content While
SPIRITUALLY SINGLE

Living the Life God Intented Is More Than Survival

Sheryl Sanderson

Acknowledgements

Thank you to those who took the time to respond to my request to share from their experiences. I am extremely grateful that they chose to open their lives by revealing their intimate thoughts and struggles of being spiritually single. I appreciate their willingness to expose their lives to help others learn from their experience. May God bless each of them abundantly.

Thank you to my husband, Russell. Thank you for your encouragement, your love, and your editing advice. Thank you for the freedom to share from our experience to help and encourage others to find their contentment in our Lord.

Thank you most of all to our Lord. In particular, I thank you for allowing me to write this book. I trust you, Lord, to put it into the hands of those whom it may help. I trust you will direct them as they delve into the Times of Reflection and know that you are waiting for them to enter into intimacy with you.

There is a time for everything,
and a season for every activity under the heavens:

a time to be born and a time to die,
a time to plant and a time to uproot,
a time to kill and a time to heal,
a time to tear down and a time to build,
a time to weep and a time to laugh,
a time to mourn and a time to dance,
a time to scatter stones and a time to gather them,
a time to embrace and a time to refrain from embracing,
a time to search and a time to give up,
a time to keep and a time to throw away,
a time to tear and a time to mend,
a time to be silent and a time to speak,
a time to love and a time to hate,
a time for war and a time for peace.

What do workers gain from their toil? I have seen the burden God has laid on the human race. He has made everything beautiful in its time. He has also set eternity in the human heart; yet no one can fathom what God has done from beginning to end. I know that there is nothing better for people than to be happy and to do good while they live. That each of them may eat and drink, and find satisfaction in all their toil—this is the gift of God. I know that everything God does will endure forever; nothing can be added to it and nothing taken from it. God does it so that people will fear him.
(Ecclesiastes 3:1–14)

Contents

Who is Spiritually Single?

The term "spiritually single" refers to anyone who has a spiritual belief system (in this case, Christianity) and does not have a spouse with which to share his or her beliefs. It may be someone not married at this time, or someone who is married to a nonbeliever, which may include someone with a different religious belief system.

MY STORY

How did I find myself spiritually single? When I met my husband in our late teen years, we were both from a background of churchgoers. We fell in love, and when we got married we did so in a church. I eventually began to draw closer to the Lord and my spouse did not choose that same path in my timing. I was married, but spiritually single for about twenty years.

When I met my husband, I knew there was a God, because that is what I had been taught. I also knew many Bible stories because I had been blessed with opportunities to attend Sunday School and other church children's programs as a child. I continued to attend church whenever I was near my parents' church. There were nice people there, and it seemed like the right thing to do. I felt a stirring in my heart during this time, and I chose to be baptized. It would be years before I awakened to the truth of what Christianity really was.

My husband and I eventually bought a home in the suburbs near my family. I again began to attend my parents' church. We started a family, and with the birth of our first child I knew there was more to this spiritual thing than I understood. It was at this time that a new minister came to our church. I responded to this minister's method of leadership and teaching. Soon the Holy Spirit began an awaking within me, giving me an understanding of the word.

My husband and I moved again into a home that was too far away to continue at that church. In hindsight, I can see several things that had to be the hand of God in that move. One is that for the first time I had to find a church on my own. I had to rely on God's, not my parents', leading.

I soon found myself with two young children and a husband who had decided he was not a Christian. This is when I realized I was spiritually single. I was horrified to realize that I was responsible for raising our children with the same opportunity to learn about Jesus as I had been provided. I felt all alone. It was then that I felt the Lord (which I would later understand to be the Holy Spirit) assure me that He was with me. In fact, I was told that our sons were not ours, but that they belonged to Him. My husband and I had only been given these children to help raise them in this world.

We did successfully raise two sons who became Christians

as children and are now godly men themselves. After they left home, my husband accepted Jesus Christ into his heart and is now a spirit-filled Christian.

OTHER SPIRITUALLY SINGLE STORIES

My story will not be your story. Each one of us will have a different path. In preparation for writing this book, I drew on the experiences of many other spiritually single people who graciously shared their intimate thoughts on their walk. Some have never been married, some are unevenly yoked to non-Christians, and others have been married but are now walking a spiritually single path for a variety of reasons.

THIS BOOK

Now to let you know what this book is not. This book does not include five easy steps to finding a Christian husband or wife. Nor is this book about five easy steps to "making" your spouse become a Christian. This book is not specifically about getting you out of the spiritually single category.

My hope is that you find your own story somewhere within these situations and take encouragement from what you read. There *"is a time for everything"* (Ecclesiastes 3:1), and for this time you are spiritually single. We will look at the challenges, blessings, and strategies of being in this situation. We will also look towards finding your purpose and contentment in life now.

> *I know that there is nothing better for people than to be happy and to do good while they live. That each of them may eat and drink, and find satisfaction in all their toil—this is the gift of God.* (Ecclesiastes, 3:12–13)

Part One

Aspects of Being
Spiritually Single

Chapter One

Challenges of Being Spiritually Single

And we know that in all things God works for the good of those who love him, who have been called according to his purpose. (Romans 8:28)

There are many challenges to being spiritually single. At times, it seems just so unfair of God to leave you all alone. After all, Psalm 37:4 says, *"Take delight in the Lord, and he will give you the desires of your heart."* For most of you reading this book, that desire includes a Christian spouse.

Let us look at some of the common complaints about being spiritually single. They generally fall into two categories. One category applies to our earthly needs, and the other to our spiritual nature. Of course, we cannot cut one area off from the other. Our earthly needs influence our spiritual lives, and our spiritual development affects our earthly walks.

Here are a few of the main aspects revealed.

LONELINESS

Being single in a couple's world can be very lonely. It can also be very lonely in a Christian circle when you are married to a non-Christian spouse. It is difficult to go to functions alone. Whether it is church events, holidays, family celebrations, or just social outings (like going to a movie), singleness can be challenging. Wedding celebrations have to be among the toughest. There are many doubts. Do you not bother going? Do you show just up on time or a little late? Where will you sit? Will anyone talk to you and ask you to join them?

You may not feel the same connection with your friends as they marry and have children. Although they may not intend to, you may feel them slowly pull away as their focus turns to their families. Then, when you do interact with them, their conversation and focus may seem to be more about their family than the fun things you used to share.

On the other end of the spectrum, you may have once been married to a Christian spouse but your circumstances have changed. If your change has happened through separation or divorce, you may feel shame or guilt; a change has occurred in how you interact with couples and families you once knew when you were "together." Or perhaps your spouse has passed away; along with your grief, you face the difficulty of re-establishing your relationships from the perspective of a single person rather than a couple.

PHYSICAL AND EMOTIONAL

Physically and emotionally, the lack of intimacy can be painful. Whether you have had a Christian partner in the past or not, you may struggle with making major decisions alone.

The ache of missing that special someone who was your confidant and prayer partner can seem daunting. You may long for times in the past when you had someone to fill those needs. Or you may ask, "Why has it not worked out for me like it has for others?" The enemy may begin to attack the mind. "What is wrong with me? How can I meet someone who makes me feel special? Is it wrong for me to want to feel loved?" If you are unevenly yoked, there is the shame and guilt of not being able to successfully witness to your spouse. If you previously had a Christian spouse and now, for whatever reason, you are on your own, you may face questions like, "Why me? Why now? Is this the way it will always be?"

SPIRITUALLY

You may wonder where God is taking you. What is your purpose? Who will pray with you? Who is close enough to discuss scripture with? How do you fulfill your responsibilities and become a person of influence without a companion?

For those who are unevenly yoked, your questions may be, "How can I submit to my husband lovingly and still hold on to my belief? What will happen if my spouse dies before receiving Christ? How can I spiritually connect with my spouse if he or she is not a Christian?" If you have children, you may ask yourself, "How can I raise my children to know Jesus if my spouse is a nonbeliever?"

You cannot wave your magic wand and make all, or any, of these issues change to what you think would be right if only you had a Christian spouse. In fact, if and when that time arrives, it may not be exactly what you imagine. But you can decide on what your attitude will be. How can you be content and trust that God has good intentions for you now, not just some time in the future? We will look at some practical strategies in Chapter Three, but first let us look at some of the blessings you may glean while you are spiritually single.

TIME OF REFLECTION

You probably will have related to some of the difficulties mentioned. You may even have thought of other difficulties not included here.

1.   Take some time to make a list of your main challenges or difficulties in being spiritually single. You do not have to list everything. Nobody has a perfect life. The purpose of this exercise is not to create greater despair, but to help you really focus on where you need the most insight. In later chapters, we are going to look further into how to deal with these challenges.

2.   Spend time in prayer. Ask the Lord for His peace in this regard. Ask Him to prepare your heart to hear what it is He is saying to you as you continue reading His word (the Bible) and this book.

3.   Before moving on to the next chapter, make another list of all the blessings or benefits you are experiencing while being spiritually single.

Chapter Two

Blessing in Being Spiritually Single

I would like you to be free from concern. An unmarried man is concerned about the Lord's affairs—how he can please the Lord. But a married man is concerned about the affairs of this world—how he can please his wife—and his interests are divided. An unmarried woman or virgin is concerned about the Lord's affairs: Her aim is to be devoted to the Lord in both body and spirit. But a married woman is concerned about the affairs of this world—how she can please her husband. I am saying this for your own good, not to restrict you, but that you may live in a right way in undivided devotion to the Lord. (1 Corinthians 7:32–35)

In quoting the above verse, I am in no way telling you to accept your fate and be grateful for it. As the Apostle Paul suggested, some people are called to remain single and are content to do so. However, the fact that you have picked up this book and read this far is an indication that you do not fall into that category. That does not make you less holy, spiritual, or worthy than the next person. Jesus loves you personally and wants you to be blessed and to enjoy your life here on earth. God did not put you here just to torment you or teach you to survive.

Well then, what are the benefits or blessings of being spiritually single? The most common response to this question is "None!" Upon further reflection, though, benefits begin to be revealed.

Mostly, these benefits are related to developing a stronger relationship with the Lord than what otherwise might be. As the Apostle Paul explained, if you are single, your time is not as divided or distracted by the practical aspects of life. People I interviewed indicated that by being single, they had more time to spend alone with the Lord. It provides motivation to diligently focus on their own walk with the Lord and a necessity to remain sensitive to His voice. They believe they have learned, and are continuing to learn, to rely more strongly on Jesus Christ.

They also indicated feeling freer to pursue God's call on their lives in various ways, including their time and money. These include such things as having more time and flexibility to minister and witness to others. One person reported feeling called to model a Christian lifestyle to other Christians.

Someone revealed that by being single, they were blessed by at least being spared the heartbreak of living with an unbeliever. Truly some would find that burden too much to bear. There is wisdom in purposing not to get involved in a relationship that would create a situation of being unequally yoked. The Apostle Paul teaches on this in 2 Corinthians 6. Please note that the

Apostle Paul was not teaching specifically on marriage, but on all relationships. This is not to say we must completely isolate ourselves from nonbelievers, for how could we otherwise effectively witness to them? Rather, we are not to get emotionally (romantically) involved.

If you are already married to a nonbeliever, do not take this as a discouragement or criticism. We will look more specifically at your situation in a future chapter. The Bible clearly tells us not to abandon a relationship if we are already married to a non-Christian.

> *To the rest I say this (I, not the Lord): If any brother has a wife who is not a believer and she is willing to live with him, he must not divorce her. And if a woman has a husband who is not a believer and he is willing to live with her, she must not divorce him. For the unbelieving husband has been sanctified through his wife, and the unbelieving wife has been sanctified through her believing husband. Otherwise your children would be unclean, but as it is, they are holy.* (1 Corinthians 7:12–14)

For those of you who have been married to a Christian and now find yourself alone, take heart in knowing that no one can take from you that blessing, or the good memories. Be encouraged that Jesus knows the ache of your heart, and He is there to walk beside you and be your helpmate. You now face the same realities of those discussed at the beginning of the chapter. Whether you remain single or not, there are blessings in the here and now. Allow the Holy Spirit to guide you along this journey.

TIME OF REFLECTION

1. Take the time look at your list of blessings or benefits of being spiritually single from the last chapter. Upon further reflection, are there any items you wish to cross off, add, or modify?

2. List some of your major giftings and talents. You don't have to share your list with anyone else if you don't want to.

3. Consider the list you just made, and your list of blessings. Look at your initial list of challenges and consider what strategies you could use to cope or change their burden.

4. Prayer time: Thank the Lord for your many blessings. Be specific. Ask Him to reveal to you how He would have you use those blessings to do His work. Thank Him for His provision in your life. Take time to stop and just bask in His love for you.

Chapter Three

Meeting Your Needs While Being Spiritually Single–Strategies

These were all commended for their faith, yet none of them received what had been promised, since God had planned something better for us so that only together with us would they be made perfect. (Hebrews 11:39–40)

WHY ARE YOU SPIRITUALLY SINGLE? WHO KNOWS?

For my thoughts are not your thoughts, neither are your ways my ways," declares the Lord. "As the heavens are higher than the earth, so are my ways higher than your ways and my thoughts than your thoughts. (Isaiah 55:8–9)

Be encouraged that God's ways are even better than what you might plan for yourself. The fact is, right now you are spiritually single. Now, what are you going to do about it?

Hopefully you have drawn some insights of your own already. I will share some strategies applied by others in hopes that you will find new strategies that apply to your situation.

In Chapter One, we talked about the challenges one can face when being spiritually single. When I asked how others filled that need, I received at least as many suggestions as there were people asked. The constant point was that they looked at their resources or blessings, and they used them as best they could to alleviate their challenges.

Some people were blessed with a close extended family. They recognized their family's willingness to always be there for them. Recognizing that fact can give you a sense of peace and belonging even if you do not always avail yourself of their help. Those things that appear overwhelming somehow become manageable knowing that you have someone who is there for you if you need them. Just knowing you are loved and cared for can put the enemy's taunts at bay.

Others drew on their church family or other Christian friends. They found someone to hook up with to attend events or share leisure time with. They found it helpful to have a Christian friend or friends to be accountable to. One person mentioned seeking out individual older Christians and asking them to be their mentors. If you are meeting on a one-on-one basis, it does not matter if that person is spiritually single or not. (By choosing older mentors, this person found their conversations did not revolve only around children and family.) Remember that to have a friend, you must be a friend.

Several people mentioned *choosing* to invest in close Christian friendships. Notice that it is a choice. It takes effort and determination to reach out to others. You will need to look for a way to contact and connect with others. Perhaps you could start a club. Some obvious ideas might be to join a Bible study group, divorce care group, young adults group, seniors group, a sports group, an arts or craft group, or any other special interest you may have. Join more than one group if they are available.

Perhaps you might initiate activities. Before starting your own group, sit down and think about what activity you really enjoy and would like to share with others. Think about who you might invite. Do they have to be single? Plan ahead for how and when you will meet. Put the idea out there, but be specific. Make a list of individuals you know who share an interest in your chosen activity. Contact them individually and specifically ask if they would like to join you. Be prepared for disappointments. Not everyone will be willing or able to join you. Do not take it personally, but move on to the next person.

One person I interviewed commented that it is important to take courage and "accept social invitations even though you may feel like the odd one out. If you don't accept, they will stop asking, and then loneliness and self-pity have a door to enter." Another person wisely questioned that if you always do what you have always done, how do you expect anything to change?

How about volunteer work, both in and outside the church? Choose volunteer activities that promote interaction with others rather than isolation. For example, help out at the food bank rather than stuffing envelopes at home.

Some other strategies for self-help are: regular Bible reading, drawing close to the Lord in prayer and praise, journaling, and making extra time to spend with Jesus.

No two stories have the same path or ending, but consider this email forward I received. Unfortunately, the author is unknown.

Consumed by my loss, I didn't notice the hardness of the pew where I sat. I was at the funeral of my dearest friend—my mother. She had finally lost her long battle with cancer. The hurt was so intense; I found it hard to breathe at times.

Always supportive, Mother had clapped loudest at my school plays, held a box of tissues while listening to my first heartbreak, comforted me at my father's death, encouraged me in college, and prayed for me my entire life. When Mother's illness was diagnosed, my sister had a new baby and my brother had recently married his childhood sweetheart, so it fell on me, the twenty-seven-year-old middle child without entanglements to take care of her. I counted it an honour.

"What now, Lord?" I asked, sitting in the church. My life stretched out before me as an empty abyss. My brother sat stoically with his face toward the cross while clutching his wife's hand. My sister sat slumped against her husband's shoulder, his arms around her as she cradled their child.

Everyone was so deeply grieving that no one noticed I sat alone. My place had been with our mother, preparing her meals, helping her walk, taking her to the doctor, seeing to her medication, reading the Bible together. Now she was with the Lord. My work was finished, and I was alone.

I heard a door open and slam shut at the back of the church. Quick footsteps hurried along the carpeted floor.

An exasperated young man looked around briefly, then sat next to me. He folded his hands and placed them on his lap. His eyes were brimming with tears. He began to sniffle.

"I'm late," he explained, *though no explanation was necessary. After several eulogies, he leaned over and commented, "Why do they keep calling Mary by the name of 'Margaret'?"*

"Because that was her name," I whispered. "Margaret. Never Mary. No one called her Mary."

I wondered why this person couldn't have sat on the other side of the church. He had interrupted my grieving with his tears and fidgeting. Who was this stranger, anyway?

"No," he insisted as several people glanced over at us. "Her name is Mary. Mary Peters."

"That isn't who this is."

"Isn't this the Lutheran church?"

"No, the Lutheran church is across the street."

"Oh."

"I believe you're at the wrong funeral, sir."

The solemnity of the occasion, mixed with the realization of the man's mistake, bubbled up inside me and came out as laughter. I cupped my hands over my face, hoping it would be interpreted as sobs.

The creaking pew gave me away. Sharp looks from other mourners only made the situation seem more hilarious. I peeked at the bewildered, misguided man beside me. He was laughing, too, as he glanced around, deciding it was too late for an uneventful exit.

I imagined Mother laughing. At the final "Amen," we darted out a door and into the parking lot.

"I do believe we'll be the talk of the town," he said with a smile. His name was Rick and since he had missed his aunt's funeral, he asked me out for a cup of coffee.

That afternoon began a lifelong journey with this man who had attended the wrong funeral but was nonetheless in the right place. A year after our meeting, we were married at a country church where he was the assistant pastor. This time, we both arrived at the same church, right on time.

In my time of sorrow, God gave me laughter. In place of loneliness, God gave me love. This past June, we celebrated our twenty-second wedding anniversary. Whenever anyone asks us how we met, Rick tells them, "Her mother and my Aunt Mary introduced us, and it's truly a match made in heaven."

Remember, God doesn't make mistakes. He puts us where we are supposed to be.

Another important point came from a person who realized she was not incomplete by being spiritually single. She chose to continue with her plans, believing God would bring the right person to cross her path, rather than spending all her time and energy looking for the right person on another path.

Your story will have a different path, and perhaps a different ending. I was praying for healing one day when I felt the Lord say to me, "Will you be content in me if you are not healed from this illness?" Now, I ask you to consider, will you be content with Jesus if you never find yourself married to a Christian?

TIME OF REFLECTION

1. Take the time to really meditate on that last question. Not *can*, but *will* you be content with Jesus even in your singleness?

2. Do a word study of the Bible, looking for scriptures that encourage you to trust that the Lord will meet or change your desires, surpassing your imagination as you keep your focus on Him.

3. Select a few key verses and memorize them to draw on in times of discouragement.

Chapter Four

Unevenly Yoked

For the unbelieving husband has been sanctified through his wife, and the unbelieving wife has been sanctified through her believing husband. Otherwise your children would be unclean, but as it is, they are holy.
(1 Corinthians 7:14)

How reassuring this verse is! Do you believe it to be true? We are told,

All Scripture is inspired by God and is useful to teach us what is true and to make us realize what is wrong in our lives. It corrects us when we are wrong and teaches us to do what is right. (2 Timothy 3:16, NLT)

That inspiration of God would include this very verse. Allow it to bring you peace.

That being said, being married to a non-Christian brings on some additional concerns. We will now take a look at a few specific questions or concerns.

1. HOW CAN I SUBMIT TO MY HUSBAND/HONOUR MY WIFE AND STILL HOLD ON TO MY BELIEF?

The answer to this question is lovingly and respectfully stated:

> *Wives, in the same way submit yourselves to your own husbands so that, if any of them do not believe the word, they may be won over without words by the behavior of their wives, when they see the purity and reverence of your lives.* (1 Peter 3:1–2)

Does your spouse object to Bibles and Christian literature being left around where they might notice and read it? Then don't do that. Have a private place you agree upon where you can keep your material for your own enjoyment and edification. Does your spouse accuse you of spending all your time at church? Consider how much time you do spend there and what events you could forgo for your spouse's benefit. Maybe you could attend events that don't interfere with your time together. Perhaps you could agree to attend events while they are busy elsewhere, such as at work or sports events you don't share. If you respect their concerns, then when there is a special event that may conflict with your time with them, they will perhaps be more supportive of you attending it.

Can you discuss their objections in order to understand what it is they object to, with the goal of reaching mutually acceptable compromises? Please note that I am not suggesting you comprise your faith, just your expression of that faith in a respectful manner. In return, you will likely find that your spouse will soften their objections and attacks on your beliefs.

I also suggest that you be mindful of your spouse's concerns, but that you focus on living out your faith in a manner that attracts rather than repels.

2. What will happen if my spouse dies before receiving Christ?

Please read the opening verse to this chapter again. Your spouse has been sanctified. Now, let me remind you that God is in control, not you. I do not mean that in a condemning way, but as a release from fear and the burden of having to *make* your spouse a believer. This one is between them and God. John 3:16 says, *"For God so loved the world that he gave his one and only Son, that whoever believes in him shall not perish but have eternal life."* Don't write your own stories (endings). You do not know what the future will bring; only God does. If you must think about the future instead of the here and now, trust God's promises.

3. How can I spiritually connect with my spouse if they are not a Christian?

Spirituality is a very powerful part of our being. It is quite natural to want to be in agreement with your spouse on spiritual matters. Everyone has a belief system, even if they do not recognize it as such. Think about this for a minute. It takes a lot of faith to believe that this world just happened, that each person is a random set of pieces that happen to go together to form a person. Your spouse has faith in something whether they know it or not. Remember also that most established faiths are of good intent. If your spouse has a different faith than yours, it is not likely to be spiteful. Move towards strengthening your relationship and living a Christ-like life by being respectful and loving despite your different beliefs at this time.

Spiritual intimacy is about more than being in agreement about every aspect of your belief system. Even couples who are both Christian often are not at the same place in their faith. Spiritual intimacy is about more than being in total agreement in a belief system; it's also about sharing your spiritual experiences.

To better understand one another's positions, you may want to embark on some of the following discussions. If you are not at a place where you can discuss these matters, contemplate on your own about what you know. Discuss, or at least think about, your birth families' backgrounds. What celebrations are recognized and how are they celebrated? How does each of you see those traditions in your current relationship? Which of these traditions are important to each of you? In what way are you able to honour both spouses' spiritual expressions without compromising your own faith?

What spiritual experiences have you shared? Have you enjoyed the wonder of a beautiful sunset together? What about other wonders of nature, the birth of a child, or just feeling blessed by your love for each other? I am sure that with some thought you could add many more personal experiences to this list.

How much is your spouse willing to accommodate your spiritual needs? Can you still pray out loud or silently in front of them? If so, do you do so gratefully and thankfully? Can you pray together? They may not be sure of their faith, but throughout the Bible we read about people referring to the God of Fill-in-the-Blank. For example, in Acts 3:13, *"The God of Abraham, Isaac and Jacob, the God of our fathers, has glorified his servant Jesus."* Is your spouse willing to pray to the God of Your Name in areas of concern?

4. I am so ashamed and/or guilty that I have a non-Christian spouse.

Where does that shame or guilt come from? Has another person challenged you on this issue? If so, who gave them the authority to place that burden on you? Is it really your own internal struggle? Since we have been made righteous in Jesus Christ, God does not condemn us. Romans 8:1 says, *"Therefore, there is now no condemnation for those who are in Christ Jesus."* Therefore, I would suggest those condemning thoughts are the lies of the enemy. God may convict us if our thoughts or actions place a stumbling stone in front of others, but He will not condemn us. If God convicts us, He will also direct us in repentance and correction. Do not blame yourself for someone else's spiritual choice. It is time to forgive and release yourself.

Each couple will have their own personality and ways of interacting. Each nonbeliever will be at their own point in their walk towards receiving salvation. Some may be hostile, some may be doubtful, some may appear not to care. It will be up to you, the believer, to be sensitive to what the Holy Spirit is saying to you about when and what to say or not say, do or not do. It is *not* up to you to *make* your spouse believe. That is between them and God.

Should you continue to model your faith to them? Absolutely! Should you continue to pray for their understanding and salvation? Absolutely! Should you be prepared to answer their questions and share with them when the opportunity arrives? Absolutely! Should you scheme and plan to manipulate situations to trick them into "getting it"? Absolutely not. Should you demand they participate in Christian teaching (TV programs, books, church, etc.)? Absolutely not.

Have you thought about how you would feel if someone else ends up leading your spouse to the Lord? Interesting thought. What would be your reaction? Yes, it would be a glorious day no matter what, but what would your thoughts be? Do you pray for other Christian friendships and influence in their lives? Matthew 9:37–38 says,

> *Then he said to his disciples, "The harvest is plentiful but the workers are few. Ask the Lord of the harvest, therefore, to send out workers into his harvest field."*

Pray that God sends other Christians into the life of your spouse. Only God knows the timing and situation of the moment your spouse receives their salvation.

OTHER FOOD FOR THOUGHT

Why does your heart long for your spouse to know Jesus? Is your heart's desire really just about your spouse's salvation? Could it about your needs? Do you long for someone to go to church functions with you? Maybe you are looking for God's clearance for the relationship decision you have made. Maybe you just don't want to look like an ineffective Christian if you can't even witness successfully to your own spouse. Is it because you are worried about their influence on your children's decisions about their faith? You may have other thoughts or concerns. My point here is that you should check your motivation.

What other effect may your spouse's salvation have on your life? No one can predetermine this, but what are some things you might ask the Lord to prepare you for? Will it change your finances, lifestyle, activities, or friendships?

What things are you putting off until your spouse becomes a Christian? Is one of those things your happiness? If so, is that really appropriate? Is that not placing too much responsibility on someone else?

TIME OF REFLECTION

1. In what ways does your spouse support your faith? What are their objections to your expression of faith? In what ways can you accommodate their concerns without compromising your faith? Start with one or two changes at a time.

2. What does spirituality mean to you? What spiritual things do you and your spouse share? What spiritual aspects of your spouse's belief are you able to share without compromising your faith? What aspects of your faith does your spouse share and/or support?

3. Is there something you are waiting to do when your spouse becomes a Christian that you could be dealing with now?

4. How might the way you pray for your spouse have changed? What prayers have already been answered?

Raising Children

Here I am, and the children God has given me. (Isaiah 8:18, Hebrews 2:13)

1. HOW CAN I RAISE MY CHILDREN TO KNOW JESUS IF MY SPOUSE IS A NONBELIEVER?

There is no simple answer to this critical question. Each person and each couple will have different responses. Ultimately, you and the Lord will have to work this out together. I will, however, share a few things from my own experience.

I endeavoured to provide a God-centred home. I made sure to continue to develop my own spiritual walk. I also endeavoured to provide good Christian instruction to my children at home and through our church.

Taking responsibility for my own spiritual development was of great importance if I was to be the spiritual leader in my home. I worked out some of the other issues we have discussed in previous chapters. When the children were very young, I admit they probably did not see me read the Bible very much, as I usually did so at a quiet time when they were not around. However, they knew I had a Bible by my bed, went to Bible studies, and to church on Sundays.

At home, I was able to have children's Bible storybooks mixed in with the rest of our children's books. My husband did not object to the material and I was able to read these books to our children in the same way I would read any other book to them. Nor would my husband object if one of our sons brought a Bible storybook to him and asked him to read it. It was perhaps just a story to their dad, but they were being exposed to a Christian foundation.

I also started prayer time with our sons at bedtime and before dinner. Again, my husband did not object, and would even remind our sons to say their prayers if he was supervising their activities. Their dad may not have prayed himself, but he honoured my desire to have our sons do so. When one of our children woke frightened at night, we prayed. If one of them got hurt, I would console them, and we would pray. If they were experiencing difficulties with another child, we would talk about the situation, and then we would pray.

From the time my children were infants, I awoke on Sunday mornings, dressed my children, fed them breakfast, and prepared for church. In my case, if my shift-worker husband was home, he would do whatever I needed to help me do so; he just did not go with me.

I will always remember one Sunday when I did all this and got to church only to find that there was no one available in the nursery to take care of my babies (an infant and a toddler). I had to do it myself. On top of that, the nursery's speaker system, meant to allow people there to hear the service, was broken. I sat there in despair, wondering why I was bothering. That is when the Lord said to me, "You take care of the spiritual needs of your family, and I will take care of yours." Within minutes, a woman came into the nursery to pass through to the office. She found me there and declared that someone should be available to take care of my children. From that Sunday on, she arranged to have a caregiver available so that I could partake in the service. God provided for my need.

When my children were a little older, they began Sunday School. As a Christian, and a teacher, my children's spiritual education was important to me. I began to take my turn as a Sunday School teacher. I taught on a rotational basis so that I could attend service sometimes, and sit under someone else's spiritual instruction.

Soon an adult male began to donate his time to the preschool Sunday School. Since I have sons, I thanked God for a Christian male influence in their lives. From that point on, many valuable Christian males were involved in my sons' church and personal lives as role models and spiritual leaders. God provided for my need before I recognized what that need was. My role was to provide the opportunities by getting them to church in the first place. In my situation, both of my sons received their salvation and were baptized at an early age.

Then came the time when they were to move from children's Sunday School to a Christian youth program. My church's youth program ran on Friday nights. I forced both of my children to attend this program. Yes, I said "forced." Each Friday night for the first little while, my sons declared that they didn't want to go. I insisted. Each Friday night, they would come home and exclaim how much fun it had been and that they wanted to go again. By the next Friday, their insecurities would convince them again that they didn't want to go. I would insist, and the cycle repeated itself. It wasn't long before my influence was no longer needed. In my first son's case, two people—a friend and a youth leader—called him every week and asked him to come. God's provision again. With my second son, he was able to go with his brother and his brother's friend. The friend's father made sure he was available to drive them. God provided.

Both of my sons still have a relationship with the Lord. In fact, one of my sons is now a youth pastor himself. God provided for our needs.

2. HOW CAN I RAISE MY CHILDREN TO KNOW JESUS IF I AM A SINGLE PARENT?

Again, there is no simple answer. Each person will have different responses to this question. Ultimately, like the unevenly yoked parent, you and the Lord will have to work this out together.

The same principles apply, in that you will need to create a God-centred home, take care of your own spiritual development, provide spiritual teaching, and trust in God to provide for your needs.

The bonus in this situation is that you will be freer to express your relationship with Jesus and trust in God. The downside is that, like any other aspect of raising your children alone, it will be up to you.

TIME OF REFLECTION

1.   In what ways are you already providing for your own spiritual development? Do you need to make any changes? Be specific.

2.   In what ways are you already providing for your children's spiritual development? Are there any things you might need to do differently or in addition? Are there other people you can call upon to help in this endeavour?

3.   In what ways is God providing for your and your children's needs for spiritual development? Have you thanked Him?

Chapter Six

Tithing

TIME, ENERGY, AND MONEY

A tithe of everything from the land, whether grain from the soil or fruit from the trees, belongs to the Lord; it is holy to the Lord. (Leviticus 27:30)

As you can tell by the title of this chapter, I apply the concept of tithing to more than just money. This is in part because of my background of being spiritually single for many years. It can be a sensitive topic. Ultimately, tithing is a decision between you and God. No person can give you the "right" answer.

Firstly, please note that the word "tithe" comes from the Old English word *teogoba*, meaning "tenth." It is defined as the one-tenth part of something. I also personally believe that I cannot make an offering towards any special ministry until I have fulfilled my tithing commitment.

At the end of this chapter, you will be given some direction in assessing your own position.

Money

We will begin with the most common form of tithing: money. If you are single, then the concepts of tithing will not be any different for you than it would be for anyone else. If you are married, this may be an area of special concern.

Before you read any further, I would suggest you give some thought to what your beliefs are in regard to tithing. Make a few notes to refer to later.

Have you ever heard, or thought, "But I don't have any money left after paying all my bills"? Consider Matthew 6:21, which says, *"For where your treasure is, there your heart will be also."*

If you are truly putting God first in your life, and you are in alignment with His will, how does the above statement apply? Take time to think about how well you are doing with your tithes at this time. Are you meeting or exceeding what the word of God instructs? Malachi 3:8 asks, *"How are we robbing you?"* and the answer is *"In tithes and offerings."*

Take heart! It is not all bad news! There are also great promises for us:

> *"Bring the whole tithe into the storehouse, that there may be food in my house. Test me in this," says the Lord Almighty, "and see if I will not throw open the floodgates of heaven and pour out so much blessing that there will not be room enough to store it."* (Malachi 3:10)

The Lord knows what your needs and desires are. He is not unaware of your income and expenses. He is not ignorant of your time commitments. He is not surprised by a crisis that may present itself to you. Go ahead and test God by bringing your whole tithe into His storehouse. Present to Him your "first fruits." Then, watch for the blessings that flow into your lives.

I have a question for you. Have you determined your opinions on tithing on your own, or have you consulted God? Have you asked for His direction on how you earn or spend your income? Whose money is it, anyway? In most situations, you have worked hard for the income you receive. Who has provided those opportunities for you? The honest answer is, obviously, God.

Consider these verses as you sit down to consider your tithing.

Now the law requires the descendants of Levi who became priests to collect a tenth from the people. (Hebrews 7:5)

Each of you should give what you have decided in your heart to give, not reluctantly or under compulsion, for God loves a cheerful giver. (2 Corinthians 9:7)

For where your treasure is, there your heart will be also. (Matthew 6:21)

MONEY (MARRIED TO A NON-CHRISTIAN)

If you are married, you will need to give some thought and prayer to how much you tithe. Finances are one of those areas that can create tension within a relationship. Not only can money create tension between husband and wife, but also between man and God.

It is hoped that within your marriage relationship, you have come to an understanding of how your income will be attained, and generally how it will be spent. The special consideration here is what the nonbelieving spouse's views are on money and the church. If they resent the family money being given to the church/God, then this could be a further roadblock to their salvation. Remember, God wants a cheerful giver, as 2 Corinthians 9:7 mentioned. If it is not willingly given, God does not want it or need it.

This will need to be prayerfully considered if your heart's desire does not line up with your spouse's. You need to especially consult God and be sensitive to your spouse's views. You will need to find a way that satisfies all three of you. For example, in my case, I was not a wage earner when I first faced this dilemma. I was a stay-at-home mother and my husband, gratefully, provide our income. He considered his money "our money," but I was still sensitive to the fact that he did so by choice. We discussed the topic of giving to my church and came to an agreement on what would be acceptable. He was okay with the decision, and I felt that I was making a contribution to our children's and my spiritual development. Most importantly, I felt I was being obedient to God in tithing and submitting to my husband. When I began to work part-time, we revisited our decision and came to a new agreement. When my husband received his salvation, we revisited our decision yet again.

Time and Energy

I have come to the view that tithing does not only refer to your money. What about the way you spend your time and energy? You may think, "I am a busy person. I do not have any time left to take on a ministry." Honestly? Are there some areas in your life where you are spending inappropriate time or money? How much of your time do you devote specifically to ministry? This does not necessarily need to be done entirely within the limits of your congregation's ministry. Perhaps there are ways you could demonstrate the love of Jesus in your neighbourhood, community, or the world at large. I invite you to explore the possibilities.

The next question is *what* time you give to God. I know we are to always walk with Him, but what time do you specifically set aside for God? For example, when do you do your devotions? First thing in the morning, last thing before you go to sleep, maybe after dinner? Is that the best time of your day? If you are at your best in the morning and are trying to stay awake long enough to do your devotions at night, is that giving God the best part of your day? If you believe God is asking you to get up early on a Saturday and care for the needy, are you obedient or do you make excuses? If you believe God is asking you to take your vacation time and spend it on a particular missions trip, are you obedient or do you create more excuses? Do you think God needs you to complete His work? No. Rather, He is providing you with an opportunity for your benefit. Keep in mind that Jesus told us, *"For my yoke is easy and my burden is light"* (Matthew 11:30). He is not asking too much. *"So give back to Caesar what is Caesar's, and to God what is God's"* (Matthew 22:21). Meet your earthly commitments, but do not neglect your kingdom responsibilities.

TIME AND ENERGY (MARRIED TO A NON-CHRISTIAN)

Again, special prayer and consideration need to be taken if you are married to a non-Christian. Consider your spouse's viewpoint. How much time is appropriate for church activities? Yes, God is to be our first priority, but our spouses also need to be considered.

As with the issue of money, you need to seek out your spouse's views on your time and energy commitment. If they see you always attending church or doing things for others at the expense of their needs, you will likely not be influencing them in favour of Christianity. However, it is fair to express your need and desire for the things of God. Let them know that it is important to you to make your faith a priority.

For example, you will want to set aside time for devotions. Does that have to be during the prime time you spend with your spouse? In my life, I found that the best time for devotions changed as our life situation changed. When our children were in preschool, my best time was right after I dropped them off for school and my husband was at work or sleeping. When I started back to work, the best time meant getting up a little earlier and spending time with God before I left for work. For me, it was a priority to attend church on Sunday. When possible, we would postpone other activities until after church. However, I was not totally inflexible if an event came up that required missing an occasional Sunday.

Finally,

> *Give and it will be given to you. A good measure, pressed down, shaken together and running over, will be poured into your lap. For with the measure you use, it will be measured to you.* (Luke 6:38)

TIME FOR REFLECTION

1. Refer back to your notes on your beliefs about tithing. What are your believes in regard to offerings?

2. Take some time to pray and ask the Holy Spirit to direct your thoughts in regards to your tithes and offerings.

3. Have you re-evaluated your beliefs on tithing? Would you like to make any changes to your current tithing? Write them out and begin to pray and meditate on how that will look.

Part Two

Moving Forward

Chapter Seven

Finding Your Purpose

But seek first his kingdom and his righteousness, and all these things will be given to you as well. (Matthew 6:33)

We have looked at many different aspects of being spiritually single. You have thought about the challenges, blessings, and strategies for living out that lifestyle. By now, you will have also noticed that it does not matter whether you have never been married but want to be, have previously been married and may or may not want to be again, or are currently married to a nonbeliever; you are not alone in your struggles. You are each in a unique position and God has a plan for you even now.

As this chapter's verse suggests, we are going to pursue finding your purpose. I cannot possibly give you the five easy steps to finding your purpose in life any more than I can give you five easy steps to receiving a spiritual partner. There are entire books (the best of which is the Bible itself) and many sermons on this topic. My prayer for you is that you gain some new direction and the peace of the Holy Spirit about your situation.

By all means, I would recommend seeking an intimate relationship with Jesus and waiting on the Lord in whichever ways you find most fruitful (listening and singing to worship music, reading the Bible, memorizing verses, prayer, praising the Lord, journaling, etc.). However, I am going to suggest that you not just sit and wait for that spiritual partner, or to be taken to your heavenly home. Be Christ-like now! Live out the life He has blessed you with now! Ask God to reveal His plans and purposes for you today rather than always dreaming about the future and what is not happening in your life.

Right now, you are living a spiritually single life. God knows that. Allow for your singleness to be a gift. Receive it. Be grateful for who you are and where you are at this moment. God will answer each of you as He determines best. He may do so by fulfilling your desire, or perhaps by changing the desire of your heart, but He wants to bless you.

Many are the plans in a person's heart, but it is the Lord's purpose that prevails. (Proverbs 19:21)

In Psalm 139:14, the psalmist claims, *"I praise you because I am fearfully and wonderfully made; your works are wonderful, I know that full well."* Let us look at this verse a little deeper. When you look in the mirror, what do you see? Often, we see flaws. We might think we would look better with shorter or longer legs, different coloured hair, more or less hair, etc. Do you realize what you are doing? You are critiquing God's work! How are you treating His creation?

Suppose someone gave you a rare, precious, and valuable

vase. What would you say? "Gee, thanks. Too bad the artist didn't make it this way instead. Maybe I could paint over it or change it." What would you do with it? Would you use it as a doorstop? No, you would treasure it. You would notice the incredible work and design. You would sit it in a safe place, a place of honour.

Now, think again about that image in the mirror. What did God bless you with? Look deeper. What have you been created to be inside? Look at what a wonderful job God has done! How are you using God's creation? Are you hiding your skills and abilities because you do not think they are good enough, or are you developing them to be all they were intended to be?

Pray and ask God to help you recognize the attributes and skills He has blessed you with. Ask God to help you use those gifts to shine His light into the world around you. Explore ways to honour God's creation.

Of course, the best place to find God's purpose for you is by asking Him and spending time in His word. An additional resource is to determine which spiritual gifts you have been given. There are many good spiritual gift quizzes available. Check the internet, ask your spiritual leader, or search a Christian bookstore. Find the one that works best for you.

Spiritual Gifts

This can be a somewhat confusing topic. What are the gifts? Who gets which gift? Does everyone get one? What do I have to do to get my gift, and how do I use it? Again, this topic is more than can be thoroughly covered in this book. That is why I suggest you do some further study. I will, however, provide a quick overview.

Firstly, some of the confusion comes because there are three categories of giftings. There are motivational, ministry, and manifestation gifts. Motivational gifts are the ones that prompt you from your heart to do or say the things you do. It is in your God-given personality. These gifts are given by our Father God. Ministry gifts come in the form of your calling, and they are given to you by Jesus. Manifestation gifts are supernatural and are given to you by the Holy Spirit.

MOTIVATIONAL GIFTS

We have different gifts, according to the grace given to each of us. If your gift is prophesying, then prophesy in accordance with your faith; if it is serving, then serve; if it is teaching, then teach; if it is to encourage, then give encouragement; if it is giving, then give generously; if it is to lead, do it diligently; if it is to show mercy, do it cheerfully. (Romans 12:6–8)

Let us briefly look at an example. You are at a dinner party and the host has prepared and delivered a wonderful meal. The conversation is good. Now, it is time for dessert. The host goes to the kitchen to deliver the great finale to this feast. As the host steps through the dining room door, he or she trips and drops the dessert, sending it flying. What is your first response?

Prophet: "I knew that was going to happen."

Server: Jump up and begin to gather up the pieces. Look for materials to clean it up with.

Teacher: "Next time, how do you think you could have transported that a little more securely?"

Encourager: "That is okay. I have done the same sort of thing. We don't need dessert, anyway."

Giver: "I will be right back. I will just run out to the store and buy something else."

Leader: "Joe, go get a cloth. Jane…"

Compassion: "Oh no! Don't feel bad. It wasn't your fault."

Could you find yourself? You may see yourself in more than one of these examples, but one or two will seem more obvious or immediate to you.

Thank you, Father God, for the gifting you have placed in each one of us. Amen.

MINISTRY GIFTS

But to each one of us grace has been given as Christ apportioned it. This is why it says: "When he ascended on high, he took many captives and gave gifts to his people." (What does "he ascended" mean except that he also descended to the lower, earthly regions? He who descended is the very one who ascended higher than all the heavens, in order to fill the whole universe.) So Christ himself gave the apostles, the prophets, the evangelists, the pastors and teachers… (Ephesians 4:7–11)

Your calling as an apostle, prophet, evangelist, pastor, or teacher may not, at first, seem obvious to you. Not all are called to these positions as a career. Many more are called to these roles in their everyday lives. You may get a better understanding by doing a quiz to help identify your calling. Notice the purpose of these gifts. They are:

to equip his people for works of service, so that the body of Christ may be built up until we all reach unity in the faith and in the knowledge of the Son of God and become mature, attaining to the whole measure of the fullness of Christ. (Ephesians 4:12–13)

Can you see how you are using your gifts to fulfill these purposes?

MANIFESTATION GIFTS

There are different kinds of gifts, but the same Spirit distributes them. There are different kinds of service, but the same Lord. There are different kinds of working, but in all of them and in everyone it is the same God at work. Now to each one the manifestation of the Spirit is given for the common good. To one there is given through the Spirit a message of wisdom, to another a message of knowledge by means of the same Spirit, to another faith by the same Spirit, to another gifts of healing by that one Spirit, to another miraculous powers, to another prophecy, to another distinguishing between spirits, to another speaking in different kinds of tongues, and to still another the interpretation of tongues. All these are the work of one and the same Spirit, and he distributes them to each one, just as he determines. (1 Corinthians 12:4–11)

Notice that the purpose of these gifts are *"the manifestation of the Spirit… given for the common good"* (1 Corinthians 12:7). Notice also that *"he distributes them to each one, just as he determines"* (1 Corinthians 12:11). You don't earn them, study for them, or tell Him which gift you want. These are not requested, like items on a birthday gift wish list. We would never be wise enough to determine which gift we should have when, nor to what extent. What a relief to know that the Holy Spirit is in charge of this!

Again, I would refer you to further investigate your primary giftings in consultation with the Holy Spirit through a more in-depth teaching and quiz.

What's the Purpose of My Gifts?

I would like to highlight here that the Bible tells us that everyone receives gifts. There is no prerequisite to earn it. You cannot buy it, and you do not need to be married to an equally spiritual partner. Nowhere does it say we only get the gifts at a certain age, time, or situation in our lives. All that is required is faith in Jesus and receiving what He sends us through the Holy Spirit. Romans 12 tell us that we have different gifts. This would indicate that we all have gifts. Ephesians 4:7 tells us that *"to each one of us grace has been given as Christ apportioned it."* Then, in 1 Corinthians 12:7, we read, *"Now to each one the manifestation of the Spirit is given."* It seems clear that we all get gifts. Which gifts, and how we use them, is entirely individualized, but still God-determined.

So what if you do know your giftings? What does that mean for your life? What is the point? Well, clearly we are also instructed in God's word that these gifts are not only for our own enjoyment, but for the good of others, to be in unity with other Christians, and to fullness of Christ.

As we study some characters from the Bible, it becomes obvious that age, status, and background do not matter when God moves. It is also evident that God's timing is not ours. David was but a shepherd boy when he killed the giant, Goliath. It was a young boy who gave his lunch (all he had) to feed thousands. Jacob worked for fourteen years for Rachael. Sarah and Abraham waited for ten years for the fulfillment of God's promise that they would bear a son. Ten years! That's amazing enough, but do you realize how old Sarah and Abraham were when God made the promise? Sarah was ninety years old and Abraham almost one hundred! Think of Esther the orphan. She went through some pretty traumatic experiences. Yet it was through Esther's willingness to risk her life that the entire Jewish race was saved.

I am guessing that if you had asked any of these people before their experiences what their purpose in life was, they would not have had a quick, specific answer. What was effective (probably beyond their imaginations) was their willingness to hear from God and do whatever He said, whenever He said it. They not only studied, meditated, and listened; they acted! The purpose of your God-given gifts is to use them. Enjoy them, bless others with them, and seek to further the kingdom of God with them.

FINDING YOUR CONFIDENCE IN CHRIST

Do you realize that you were created for God's pleasure? *"For the Lord takes delight in his people"* (Psalm 149:4). He wants to be a friend of yours. Yes, you! John 15:15 tells us, *"I no longer call you servants, because a servant does not know his master's business. Instead, I have called you friends."* Wow! Talk about knowing people in high places! There is no higher place!

Because of Jesus and what He did for each of us, we have the right and privilege of sitting at the Father's feet. We do not have to wait for some day in the future when we are good enough or when we wrangle permission. He has invited us to experience eternity now. The Holy Spirit will usher us into His presence through the power and grace of Jesus Christ. Well, if He has invited us in, who can stop us? Those doubts, those condemnations and accusations, those fears and feelings of worthlessness are not of God, but from the devil. John 10:10 warns us that the devil comes as a thief—*"The thief comes only to steal and kill and destroy"*—but Jesus says, *"I have come that they may have life, and have it to the full."*

So, how do you relate to a friend? Usually you enjoy spending time with them. You feel free and safe to share your thoughts and feelings. The benefit with Jesus is that you do not have to guard how much you share because He already knows it, and still loves and accepts you. You get to know your friend and enjoy doing things together. You enjoy doing things that you know your friend will like and appreciate. Hopefully your mind will not be on what is in it for you, but rather what you can do for that friend to give them pleasure, and vice versa. Well, we know that God wants to bless us.

As you spend time developing the friendship offered to you by God, you will get to know Him even better. Your confidence will be in Him, not yourself. Do you really believe Jesus when He said He would send the Holy Spirit to you? Are you willing to allow the Holy Spirit to work in your everyday life?

> *Finally, brothers and sisters, whatever is true, whatever is noble, whatever is right, whatever is pure, whatever is lovely, whatever is admirable—if anything is excellent or praiseworthy—think about such things.* (Philippians 4:8)

Focus your thoughts on what is true, good, and right. Focus your thoughts on what you can do for God, not what He can do for you. Being spiritually single is not about what you are missing out on; it's about what you can accomplish for God's kingdom now.

Sometimes it might not make sense in your mind. Sometimes it might be rather scary. Imagine how Esther felt when she heard this:

> *For if you remain silent at this time, relief and deliverance for the Jews will arise from another place, but you and your father's family will perish. And who knows but that you have come to your royal position for such a time as this?* (Esther 4:14)

Like Esther, your current situation may be *"for such a time as this."*

Ultimately, our purpose is to allow God to work through us any way He wants to bring glory to Him alone. Ephesians 2:10 declares, *"For we are God's handiwork, created in Christ Jesus to do good works, which God prepared in advance for us to do."*

TIME OF REFLECTION

1. Find and do a spiritual gifts quiz.

2. Now that you know your giftings, do you see you have already been using them? Do you see yourself using them any differently now than you have in the past?

3. How are you developing your friendship with God?

4. In what ways are you planning to continue to discover your God-planned purpose? What are you doing towards fulfilling that purpose now?

Chapter Eight

Contentment

I have learned the secret of being content in any and every situation, whether well fed or hungry, whether living in plenty or in want. I can do all this through him who gives me strength.
(Philippians 4:12–13)

WHAT IS CONTENTMENT?

Contentment is a noun that refers to a state of happiness and satisfaction. This does not mean that you go around in a constant dreamlike state of worldly joy and selfish fulfillment. ("I see it. I want it. Give it to me now.") The contentment I am referring to is about something deeper and internal, regardless of what is happening in the world around us. Furthermore, contentment is not something automatically ingrained in our makeup. It is learned. The Apostle Paul said,

> *But godliness with contentment is great gain. For we brought nothing into the world, and we can take nothing out of it. But if we have food and clothing, we will be content with that.* (1 Timothy 6:6–8)

I remember a story Luci Swindoll told at a conference I attended. It went something like this. She was set to go on a cruise. She was really looking forward to seeing penguins in their natural setting. Each day, she went out onto the deck and searched the horizon in hope that would be the day she spotted them. This went on for a few days until she suddenly realized she was so focused on searching for penguins that she was missing out on all the fun the other passengers were having. Wisely, she joined in the life going on around her and had a wonderful trip!

I am often reminded of that story in my everyday life. For example, on several scuba-diving excursions, I have been focused intently on finding something really small or hidden and neat. Then I rein myself in and look around, enjoying the absolute beauty of the underwater world just as it is.

I share these examples as a reminder not to miss the blessings and works of God in your life as you focus on your situation of being spiritually single, or some other such problem. It is perfectly alright to seek things; just do not get so focused on them that you miss out on all the other joys and rewards.

Why Do You Really Want It?

Have you ever really thought about why you want what you want? For example, why do you want a spiritual partner? Is it for God's glory, the other person's salvation, or just to fulfill all the things we talked about at the beginning of this book for *you*? What is your ultimate motive and purpose in wanting what you want? Is your life God-centred or self-centred?

> *…whatever is true… think about such things.*
> (Philippians 4:8)

Do not curse yourself with thoughts or words of "I am single, married to a non-Christian, cannot meet the right person, etc." Instead, in these matters, focus your thoughts and prayers on "When my spouse receives salvation, when I meet my future spouse, thank you, Jesus, for being my husband and provider." Act in faith now, as if your prayers have already been answered. Dwell on what is good. Trust God to take care of the rest in His perfect timing. Here are a few Bible verses about waiting on the Lord:

> *…but those who hope in the Lord will renew their strength. They will soar on wings like eagles; they will run and not grow weary, they will walk and not be faint.* (Isaiah 40:31)

> *Let us not become weary in doing good, for at the proper time we will reap a harvest if we do not give up.* (Galatians 6:9)

Enjoy that strength as you wait in expectation of the harvest.

> *Trust in the Lord and do good; dwell in the land and enjoy safe pasture. Take delight in the Lord, and he will give you the desires of your heart.* (Psalm 37:3–4)

Your role is to delight in the Lord. He will give you the desires of your heart.

> *For we are God's handiwork, created in Christ Jesus to do good works, which God prepared in advance for us to do.* (Ephesians 2:10)

We talked in the last chapter about not criticizing His work. He has already done the work of preparing what we are to do; we simply need to be obedient.

> *And we know that in all things God works for the good of those who love him, who have been called according to his purpose.* (Romans 8:28)

WHY? IT IS FOR HIS PURPOSE.

> *I know that there is nothing better for people than to be happy and to do good while they live. That each of them may eat and drink, and find satisfaction in all their toil—this is the gift of God.* (Ecclesiastes 3:12–13)

We do not understand all that God has planned. We do not even know why certain things happen, whether it is God's plan, man's choices, or Satan's attack. This verse tells us that we should endeavour to *"do good while [we] live"* and enjoy the blessings God provides for us. Why? Ecclesiastes 3:14 tells us it is so *"that people will fear [God]."*

Some people who appear to have very easy and fun jobs seem discontent. Other people whose jobs are very laborious and difficult still seem to find joy. Have you ever noticed labourers singing while they work? I remember one man whose job it was to drive those little carts around the airport, helping people who need to get from one point to another. As I sat waiting for my flight, I noticed him go back and forth, back and forth, time and again. He spent his whole shift in one little area of the airport. It does not sound very exciting, does it? This man, however, was happy. He would make a sound like an air horn and then keep a deadpan face. It was so much fun to watch people look all around to see where the sound was coming from. Once they figured it out, they would in turn watch the next group of people, and there was laughter for all.

This man was providing a service for others. He was doing it with a joyful heart. His appearance told me that he was receiving all he needed to *"eat and drink,"* although I am sure he would not have been highly paid for his labour. I do not know what challenges he may have been facing in life, but he was enjoying his gifts from God.

No matter what your days involve, or your current situation, do you enjoy God's gifts?

ARE YOU READY FOR GOD TO ANSWER YOUR PRAYER?

I want to take a brief look at something many never consider as they plead with God to answer their prayers. Are you ready for Him to answer your prayers the way you have asked? Take time to consider some of the possible effects.

For example, if you are praying for a spouse, are you ready to give up your independence? Are you ready to compromise where you live, how you celebrate holidays, or other critical aspects of your life? Are you ready to stop and take time to consult with someone else before leaping into a new endeavour or commitment? If you are praying for your spouse to receive salvation, have you considered how that will change your lifestyle? The activities you do, the friends you have, the way you spend money?

I am not trying to shoot down your desires. I am just suggesting that you prepare for all the ramifications of the answer, or at least expect the unexpected. Neither am I suggesting that it will all be negative; I am sure there will be many blessings! It is just that we as humans do not always consider the whole picture. You know the saying that says the grass is always greener on the other side of the fence? This list of considerations is not complete, and these examples may not apply to you at all, but really think about your own situation. Pray that God will reveal to you anything you need to know, or acknowledge, in regards to your desires.

PRAYER AND TRUSTING GOD

The question is not can you trust God to answer your prayers in His perfect timing, but will you? Will you accept that His answer is the best answer for you, even if it varies from your expectations? As one person shared with me, "I can still pray for what I think are my heart's desires, but at the same time I accept that where I am is God's best for me now. If it was not His best for me, He could easily change it. The more often I choose to accept my life as God has designed it, the more I am under an umbrella of grace to accept spiritual singlehood."

So what are some things you could be praying for? Pray for that spiritual partner, for your spouse's salvation, to heal the hurt or void of the spiritual partner you may have had but have now lost, or to know Jesus as that partner. Do not forget to pray for *contentment and the joy of the Lord*—the joy that is not necessarily external, but deep within. Pray that God would help you to find contentment in Him. Pray that He will direct your thoughts and remind you to choose joy. Pray that God will use your situation or experience to mould you into someone you never otherwise could have become. *"Rejoice always, pray continually, give thanks in all circumstances; for this is God's will for you in Christ Jesus"* (1 Thessalonians 5:16–18).

In Deuteronomy 16:15, we read,

> *For seven days celebrate the festival to the Lord your God at the place the Lord will choose. For the Lord your God will bless you in all your harvest and in all the work of your hands, and your joy will be complete.*

They were to worship and praise God with the promise of blessings and that their joy would be complete. In Nehemiah 8:10, the people were directed,

> *Go and enjoy choice food and sweet drinks, and send some to those who have nothing prepared. This day is holy to our Lord. Do not grieve, for the joy of the Lord is your strength.*

They were told to move into action for the Lord and not to grieve, knowing that the joy of the Lord was their strength.

Pray to recognize that joy and contentment from deep within. Be ready to live your life as God would have you do so now. Choose to be Christ-centred. Know that Jesus loves you, treasures you, is your friend, and wants what is best for you. Put your hope in Him and allow the Holy Spirit to fill you with blessings, joy, contentment, and confidence in the Lord.

TIME OF REFLECTION

1.   What are you focusing on that might be causing you to miss what God has for you now?

2.   Why do you ask God for the things you ask for?

3.   What are some things you should be ready to address when your prayer is answered? How does this affect your attitude?

4.   Will you trust God?

5.   What other verses can you find that speak of contentment and joy in the Lord? Write them out and memorize them.

Chapter Nine

Intimate Time with God

Keep this Book of the Law always on your lips; meditate on it day and night, so that you may be careful to do everything written in it. Then you will be prosperous and successful. (Joshua 1:8)

Now we come to the time of personal dedication to intimacy with God. Whether this is the first time you are seeking a deeper intimacy with the Lord, or it is just a renewing of your spiritual life, my prayer is that this is a life-changing event for you.

I have included thirty-one verses to get you started for your first month, one verse for each day. I have purposely not made any comment, just providing the verse straight out of the word of God. You might want to set aside some quiet time each day to focus on the verse and listen to what the Lord has to say to you about it. Memorize the verse, write it out and carry it around for the day to refer to often, or find your own way of using it to direct your focus on the Lord. I would encourage you to journal anything you hear the Lord impress on you, or any thoughts you have as you meditate on each verse.

I would then suggest that you start your own verse-journaling. Write out any verses you find significant. Then journal what each verse means specifically for you.

Finally, I have included a prayer for you to use. Take the parts that are meaningful to you and pray them from your heart. Add your prayers to what I have begun. Some find it useful to write their prayers out. Remember: God is your Father in heaven, Jesus is your friend, and the Holy Spirit is your messenger. Take a break in your prayers to listen for what they have to say to you.

May you find contentment in the Lord in your current life.

Day One

And we know that in all things God works for the good of those who love him, who have been called according to his purpose. (Romans 8:28)

_____

_____

_____

_____

_____

_____

_____

_____

_____

_____

_____

_____

_____

_____

_____

_____

_____

_____

_____

_____

_____

_____

_____

_____

_____

Day Two

She is clothed with strength and dignity, and she laughs without fear of the future. (Proverbs 31:25, NLT)

_____
_____
_____
_____
_____
_____
_____
_____
_____
_____
_____
_____
_____
_____
_____
_____
_____
_____
_____
_____
_____
_____
_____
_____
_____
_____
_____
_____

DAY THREE

Trust in the Lord and do good; dwell in the land and enjoy safe pasture. Take delight in the Lord, and he will give you the desires of your heart. (Psalm 37:3–4)

DAY FOUR

Give me understanding, so that I may keep your law and obey it with all my heart. Direct me in the path of your commands, for there I find delight. Turn my heart toward your statutes and not toward selfish gain.
(Psalm 119:34–36)

DAY FIVE

Listen to me, you islands; hear this, you distant nations: Before I was born the Lord called me; from my mother's womb he has spoken my name. (Isaiah 49:1)

Day Six

But you, man of God, flee from all this, and pursue righteousness, godliness, faith, love, endurance and gentleness. Fight the good fight of the faith. Take hold of the eternal life to which you were called when you made your good confession in the presence of many witnesses. (1 Timothy 6:11–12)

DAY SEVEN

I know what it is to be in need, and I know what it is to have plenty. I have learned the secret of being content in any and every situation, whether well fed or hungry, whether living in plenty or in want. (Philippians 4:12)

DAY EIGHT

So if the Son sets you free, you will be free indeed. (John 8:36)

Day Nine

Finally, brothers and sisters, whatever is true, whatever is noble, whatever is right, whatever is pure, whatever is lovely, whatever is admirable—if anything is excellent or praiseworthy—think about such things. (Philippians 4:8)

Day Ten

"Truly I tell you," Jesus said to them, "no one who has left home or wife or brothers or sisters or parents or children for the sake of the kingdom of God will fail to receive many times as much in this age, and in the age to come eternal life." (Luke 18:29–30)

Day Eleven

These were all commended for their faith, yet none of them received what had been promised, since God had planned something better for us so that only together with us would they be made perfect. (Hebrews 11:39–40)

DAY TWELVE

And my God will meet all your needs according to the riches of his glory in Christ Jesus. (Philippians 4:19)

DAY THIRTEEN

For where your treasure is, there your heart will be also. (Matthew 6:21)

Day Fourteen

And a voice from heaven said, "This is my Son, whom I love, with him I am well pleased." (Matthew 3:17)

DAY FIFTEEN

Now if you obey me fully and keep my covenant, then out of all nations you will be my treasured possession.
(Exodus 19:5)

Day Sixteen

"On the day when I act," says the Lord Almighty, "they will be my treasured possession. I will spare them, just as a father has compassion and spares his son who serves him." (Malachi 3:17)

DAY SEVENTEEN

For you are a people holy to the Lord your God. The Lord your God has chosen you out of all the peoples on the face of the earth to be his people, his treasured possession. (Deuteronomy 7:6)

Day Eighteen

"For I know the plans I have for you," declares the Lord, "plans to prosper you and not to harm you, plans to give you hope and a future." (Jeremiah 29:11)

Day Nineteen

"When you seek me in prayer and worship, you will find me available to you. If you seek me with all your heart and soul, I will make myself available to you," says the Lord. (Jeremiah 29:13–14, NET)

DAY TWENTY

But godliness with contentment is great gain.
(1 Timothy 6:6)

_____

_____

_____

_____

_____

_____

_____

_____

_____

_____

_____

_____

_____

_____

_____

_____

_____

_____

_____

_____

_____

_____

_____

_____

_____

DAY TWENTY-ONE

If they obey and serve him, they will spend the rest of their days in prosperity and their years in contentment. (Job 36:11)

Day Twenty-Two

Be strong and courageous. Do not be afraid or terrified because of them, for the Lord your God goes with you; he will never leave you nor forsake you. (Deuteronomy 31:6)

DAY TWENTY-THREE

Rejoice always, pray continually, give thanks in all circumstances; for this is God's will for you in Christ Jesus. (1 Thessalonians 5:16)

DAY TWENTY-FOUR

Then he said to his disciples, "The harvest is plentiful but the workers are few. Ask the Lord of the harvest, therefore, to send out workers into his harvest field." (Matthew 9:37–38)

DAY TWENTY-FIVE

But seek first his kingdom and his righteousness, and all these things will be given to you as well.
(Matthew 6:33)

_____

_____

_____

_____

_____

_____

_____

_____

_____

_____

_____

_____

_____

_____

_____

_____

_____

_____

_____

_____

_____

_____

_____

_____

DAY TWENTY-SIX

The Lord will vindicate me; your love, Lord, endures forever—do not abandon the works of your hands. (Psalm 138:8)

Day Twenty-Seven

For we are God's handiwork, created in Christ Jesus to do good works, which God prepared in advance for us to do. (Ephesians 2:10)

DAY TWENTY-EIGHT

Nevertheless, each person should live as a believer in whatever situation the Lord has assigned to them, just as God has called them. This is the rule I lay down in all the churches. (1 Corinthians 7:17)

Day Twenty-Nine

You make known to me the path of life; you will fill me with joy in your presence, with eternal pleasures at your right hand. (Psalm 16:11)

DAY THIRTY

In him we were also chosen, having been predestined according to the plan of him who works out everything in conformity with the purpose of his will, in order that we, who were the first to put our hope in Christ, might be for the praise of his glory. (Ephesians 1:11–12)

DAY THIRTY-ONE

The word of the Lord came to me, saying, Before I formed you in womb I knew you, before you were born I set you apart. (Jeremiah 1:4–5)

My Verses

(Any verses that have stood out or spoken to you through this study.)

_____

_____

_____

_____

_____

_____

_____

_____

_____

_____

_____

_____

_____

_____

_____

_____

_____

_____

_____

_____

_____

_____

_____

_____

_____

Prayer Time

Heavenly Father, I give You thanks for sending Your son to die for me. Forgive me, Lord, for all my sins and poor attitudes. I give thanks to You, Jesus, for being my friend even when I do not act like a friend to You. I give You thanks for sending the Holy Spirit to me as my counsellor and guide. I am so honoured by Your love, grace, and mercy. Help me to be all You have planned for me.

Thank You for being my ultimate prayer partner. Lord, I pray that You would help me recognize the people You send to me to fulfill the role of a prayer partner here on earth. Thank You for the many blessings You have already showered on me. *(List some here.)* Lord, where I have been too self-focused to notice the blessings around me, please prompt me to look up.

Thank You, Lord, that You know the desires of my heart and that You want me to be fulfilled. Lord, I would ask that You direct me to that life partner in Your perfect timing. Forgive my impatience, fears, and anxiety.

OR

Lord, thank You for the spouse You have blessed me with. Help me to always be respectful and loving towards him/her. I pray that You would give them an understanding of who You are. Give me Your spirit of wisdom to be ready to answer their questions when You so inspire. I pray for other positive Christian fellowship in their life. Give me Your peace about their salvation. I know You would not want one of Your people to miss out on their salvation. Lord, I look forward to the time when we will be united as a "cord of three."

OR

Lord, thank You for being with me in times of despair. I so miss my spouse, but I am grateful for Your comfort. Thank You for healing me. Thank You for fulfilling those things I once counted on my spouse for. Help me to recognize You in those provisions.

Lord, I thank You that You will provide good spiritual influence in my children's lives. Give me Your wisdom in providing opportunities for them to know You. Thank You for allowing me to partner with You to raise these godly men/women. I am so grateful that You watch over them and protect them even when they are beyond my reach. I trust You will give them a true understanding of who You are. I pray that You would reveal to them the lies of the enemy and the truth of who You are. Lord, shine Your light into their lives.

Holy Spirit, please direct me in regards to tithing and offerings. You know my situation. You even know where I will be in the future. Inspire me to tithe money, time, and energy as You would have me do. Lord, I want to be a cheerful giver. May my efforts further Your kingdom.

Lord, I ask You to direct my prayers. Reveal any strongholds that may be at work in my life or the lives of my loved ones. Help me to recognize the works of the enemy and to rebuke him with the power You have given me through the Holy Spirit.

I pray that I would recognize Your purpose for me in this life now. I ask that You would guide me into knowing what to do, and having my confidence in You, to be obedient. I know You have nothing but the best planned for me. Lord, I do trust you. Help me to trust my relationship with You, in that I will know Your calling. Remind me constantly to choose joy—true joy, joy that is from You. Lord, I ask You to help me be content with the plans You have for me. I pray that I would be content just in knowing You, and being known by You.

In Jesus' precious name I pray, Amen.